THE SPIRITED EARTH

THE SPIRITED EARTH

Dance, Myth, and Ritual from South Asia to the South Pacific

Photographs and text by Victoria Ginn
Foreword by Keri Hulme

RIZZOLI
NEW YORK

To the Visionary Heart, and all who cherish it

First published in the United States of America in 1990 by
Rizzoli International Publications, Inc.
300 Park Avenue South, New York, NY 10010

Library of Congress Cataloging-in-Publication Data

Ginn, Victoria.
    The spirited earth : dance, myth, and ritual from South Asia to
the South Pacific / photographs and text by Victoria Ginn;
foreword by Keri Hulme.
    Includes bibliographical references (p. 190).
    ISBN 0–8478–1167–0
    1. Dancing—Asia, South—Anthropological aspects.
2. Dancing—Oceania—Anthropological aspects.   3. Asia, South—
Social life and customs.   4. Oceania—Social life and
customs.   I. Title.
GV1588.6.G56   1990
793.3—dc20   90–34682
                                                    CIP

Set in type by Rainsford Type, Danbury, Connecticut
Printed and bound by Dai Nippon Printing Company, Tokyo, Japan
Map by Lundquist Design, New York

Design by Massimo Vignelli

Front jacket: Dummy-horse dance. Tamil Nadu, India
Back jacket: Tale from the Panji cycle, Java, Indonesia
Frontispiece: Representation of the Balinese deity Tjintiya, the
Divine Androgyne, or in India, Shiva Nataraja—Lord of the Dance.
Bali, Indonesia

Contents

ACKNOWLEDGMENTS *10*

FOREWORD *Keri Hulme* *12*

INTRODUCTION *14*

THE STORYTELLERS *18*

ARCHETYPES OF CULTURE *56*

COMMUNION AND TRANSFORMATION *98*

THE JOURNEY *136*

BIBLIOGRAPHY *190*

Acknowledgments

Among the many people who participated in my journey, assisting me along the way, I wish to thank:

In Bali: Made Kana; Njoman Kardi; Ule and Made Pering; Gede Raka Kompiang, his son, and the people of Ubud; Albert Beaucoup.

In Java: the students of Sasminta Mardawa: Rinto Widiyarto, Herni Tri Suprihati, Sriwahyum, Suivarsono, and Subandriyo; Sukasman; Jurriaan and Janine Fermansjah.

In Sumatra: Mardjami Martamin and the students of the Akedemi Seni Karawitan.

In Borneo: Simon Strickland and the Kejaman Lasah and Bidayuh people of Sarawak; Genevieve Nicol and her family.

In Thailand: Chamaiporn Buddharat, Preecha Silpasombat, Judith Sooksombatisatian and the New Zealand High Commission, Bangkok; Otome Hutheesing and the Lisu and Akha people of North Thailand.

In Burma: Mg Hla Kyi.

In India: Tenzin Gonpo; Khampa Gar Monastery; Atisha-lar and the headquarters for Tibetan Buddhism, Himachal Pradesh; Dayaram; Tulsi Ram and the Bheel community of Udaipur; Tulsi-Das Suthar; Bragha Guruswamy; C. Khisnan; the Kerala Kalamandalam and its students: Vijayakumar, Udayakumar, and Kabadharan; Prabhakar Pai; Subbanna Bhat; Krishnaswamy Jois; Perdur Rama; Harady Sanjiva; S. Laksminarayana; C. Sivadas and the Australian High Commission, New Delhi; Keshav and Komar Kothari.

In Nepal: Ram Bahadur Thapa and his family; Santi; Tashi Phalkhiel; Sane Gunly; Uttam Raj Karnikar and the Mahakali group of Bhaktapur; Damodar Shrestha.

In Australia: Topsy and her friends; Dick Darwin; Stanley Tipalora and the people of Bathurst Island; Steven Anderson; John Zeroni; the people of Peppermenarti; Stanley Nunkara; Annie and James Kalkeeyorta; Dorothy Pootchemunka; Isobel Wolmby; Clive and Lou Yunkaporta and the people of Aurukun; Wanjuk, Wayula, and Mapupu Marika; Lumin Yunnupingu; Yikuni Gurruwiwi and the people of Yirrikala; Ralph and Irwin Riley; Suzanne Holt; Isaac Hobson, Jerry Pascoe, Peter Creek, Phillip Pollow, Jessiah Omeenyo, and the children of Lockhart River.

In the Solomon Islands: Francis and Beverly Taupongi; Toomasi Taupongi; Haman Sau'eha; Tepuke Baiango; Steven Puia; Japaret Pongi; Momoka Tekehu; Abither Tangosia; Elihu Haluihi; Pollen Keiae; Jotham Taumata; Temasi Teikamua; Loise Baikaba; Ben Kiriau; William; Unuia, Faukedea, Inarobo Aumanu, and the people of Waratolo, Malaita; Reresimae Tafia and the people of Natagera; Father Abel Ta'ai; Ambrose, his family, and the people of Santa Cruz; Wilson Maelaua; Lawrence Foanaota and the Solomon Islands Museum, Guadalcanal.

In Vanuatu: Melteluch Betehule and the people of Vao; Kamai; Methas; Kambong Rantes; Albin and Plasing Rubin and the people of Malekula; Graham Jackson; Ian Wollard; Kirk Huffman and the Vanuatu Museum, Vila.

In New Zealand: Heema Tangira; Zac Wallace; Te Rautahi and Mavis Tuoro; Kelly Waenga; the New Zealand Ministry of Foreign Affairs.

And all those who let me share their earth as my mattress and stars as my blanket.

For their help with research at the end of my journey, I thank: David Martin, department of Prehistory and Anthropology, Australian National University, Canberra; William Davenport, curator of Anthropology, University Museum of Archaeology and Anthropology, Philadelphia, Pennsylvania; Arthur Mandlebaum, scholar of Tibetan Tantra, New York; Fritz De Boer, department of Theater, Wesleyan University, Middletown, Connecticut; Fox Quaina, Santa Ana, Solomon Islands; Sal Murgiyanto, scholar of Javanese dance and drama, New York; Virginia Meyers and Reverend Maori Marsden, Auckland, New Zealand; and M. Gutschow and Gert M. Wegner.

For their sponsorship, I thank: Agfa Gevaert New Zealand, Limited, Wellington; Solair-Solomon Islands Airways, Guadalcanal; Kodak New Zealand, Limited, Auckland; Queen Elizabeth II Arts Council of New Zealand, Wellington; Fay, Richwhite and Company, Limited, Auckland, New Zealand.

For their interest and assistance, my gracious thanks to: Marion Connell and her son, Martin Connell, Toronto, Canada; Alain Sayag, Centre Georges Pompidou, Paris; David Richwhite, Fay, Richwhite and Company, Limited, Auckland, New Zealand; R. M. Henderson, Lincoln Center Library for the Performing Arts, New York; Michael E. Hoffman; Nicholas Callaway; Geraldine Stutz; Jane Opper; Rohesia Hamilton Metcalf; Peter Witte; Bob Cato; Dianne Ward; Anthony Levintow; Merlin Stone; Anne Webster; Bronwyn Janes; Peter Debreceny; Deborah Tait; Vivian Lynn; Keri Hulme; Witi Ihimaera; my parents, Ellinore and Russell Ginn, and my family; Rizzoli International Publications, New York, for their interest in the subject matter of this book and the generous excellence they have granted to its design, reproduction, and overall quality. And, my editor at Rizzoli, Sarah Burns, for the clarity and structure she has brought to the text as well as her patience and persistence.

Of all the many people connected in some way or another to this book, the one who stands out is my travelling companion, Anna Crichton. An artist in her own right, Anna displayed an extraordinary generosity of spirit as well as practical assistance throughout the "making" of this book. I very much doubt that it would have been realized without her. In acknowledgment of her role in it, this book is also dedicated to the selflessness of true friendship.

TIHEI MAURIORA

IN THE BEGINNING—Tihei mauriora.
There was the god, that creative vortex of light, who already knew oppression and darkness and relentless struggle.
There was the red clay form, cunningly shaped, the outward expression of the god's inward longing, but as yet silent, and static upon the beach.
He—for the god was Tane-Mahuta-te-wairo—had tried many ways to wake the work of his hands. He had chanted, he had urged, he had danced in his light.

Finally, he leaned over the clay woman and breathed his breath into her nostrils. And she sneezed.
"Tihei mauriora! The sneeze of quintessential life!"
She was the first human being, Hine-ahu-one, the Woman-formed-of-clay. From her, and from Tane—and his great parents, Papatuanuku-Earth Mother and Ranginui-Sky Father—we all of us are sprung.

I am enchanted by the thought that the first human sound the world heard was not a baby's cry, or the guttural throbbing chant of the first priest/ess but that explosive happenstance outburst that besets us all. Uh, bless you.

Many years ago I fantasized that every sound made on this earth, and every sound made *by* Earth—from mouse-squeak to sobbing, from the zitzit of crickets to the terrifying scream of an elephant in fury, from the wrenching groaning of glaciers to the almost inaudible rippling of creek-water over sand, from the rustle of reeds to the great ocean's roar—all of these sounds combine to be Earth's voice and song.

O, I know this place rings like a gong when an earthquake strikes, and, for all I know, She may wail aloud when comets smash into her skin, but my fantasy was, and is, something different: if we could stand away from our home, far enough away, we could maybe hear it all, the anguish and the joy melded to a triumphant note.

Likewise, movement: chaotic as a spastic child, spontaneous as a dust devil, or as minutely timed and organized as an unfolding flower, *mudra*, or ballet. And bees dance informational dances; fish court in sinuous patterns; chimpanzees go noisily crazy, with a kind of terror-filled joy (which I suspect we, their cousins, know in our bones but prefer not to acknowledge as part of the commonality of apes),

12

dancing when the rains come.
And if you have ever seen the zesty acrobatic dancing of dolphins getting ready to mate or watched adolescent albatrosses gam, with strange hieratic posturings, you will know that body language, the song of the dance, rings through mind and time as loud as any shouted words.

This kinetic accompaniment, the Dance underlying the Song . . .
Imagine the Laban notation for that!
Perhaps we encode it; perhaps it is Life.
Humans seem to encode it most of all, because we seek to ritualize and celebrate and transmit insights. We seek to make sense of the world.

And sometimes—not often—there is a human around with an obsession, *a magnificent obsession*, and skill with one of our better machines, the camera, when we engage in our ancient ways to join body and song, to feed the stars, to keep the blood of the world circulating, to keep *us* continuing.
Sometimes this human with the magnificent obsession is around when there are efforts made to consecrate past pain (as in the unforgettable Mud People, cowering before the invaders but still able to dance, "We survived! WE survived!").
Or, around catching gods incarnate in the dancers, posturingly, prancingly dangerous.
Or, balanced on the perch of humanity's sullen adolescence, around to take the portrait of the whimsical and frenetic child we cannot yet outgrow.
We repress that child at our peril.

Victoria Ginn—Ginn as in *begin*, not as djinn—takes and makes such pictures.
Pictures may be mirrors
may mirror what is . . . not there
or be flighty . . . flail . . . fail
to make you see
any more than any mirror anywhere
but then again may lightly give
a perfect gift of insight
may be a life.

In a peculiarly timely way—because human cultures that identify with the old ways of Earth and Spirit seem to be in the process of becoming overwhelmed by the less compassionate, the crass, and monetarily-brutalist societies of the world—in a peculiarly timely way, Ginn has been given pictures.
Given?

Granted, she has skill with a camera; granted, with sweat and pain, she got herself to the arenas. And the multifarious peoples, with trust, offered a chance to see, and take, some of their ancestral insights and secrets.
And she was *given* pictures.
Pictures which are mirrors. Pictures which show the Earth as we dance her. Pictures of the Gods and the Child who intervene . . . and watch.

It is a cliché to say that there is more to our world than is seen; it's the kind of truism that slicks off the tongue. You say it mindlessly, yeah, yeah, more to the world than we see. If you read it, your eyes skim past, yeah, yeah, more to etc.
But it's true.

Not all of us are travellers in the sense that we enjoy going to alien lands. We are omnivorously curious about the rest of humanity, however. And while few of us are travellers in the spiritual sense, we would like to know . . .
(If you go looking for the numinous, hunting It, pursuing meanings along the many ways of God, you will not only find, you may also become the hunted, the pursued. Is "sought-after/longed for" any less terrifying?)

Within these covers is a journey, and a record. Read carefully. Mused upon, it will give you stunning insights.

For over a thousand years, the Maori of New Zealand/Aotearoa have begun speeches and prayer with that formulaic phrase.
Greetings to you, reader of *The Spirited Earth*. I salute the breath of life you breathe, we all share.

TIHEI MAURIORA!

Keri Hulme
September 1989
Okarito, New Zealand

Introduction

The image of Tjintiya or Shiva Nataraja—Lord of the Dance—opens this book as it greeted me at the beginning of my journey: "a dancing spirit" at the entrance to a mystic and mythical realm. Summoning all the powers of this most ancient of performing arts—the dance—the Hindu god Shiva Nataraja danced to life nature and all its creatures. Here, drawing on both the Hindu and even earlier Balinese concept of the deity as Tjintiya, the Divine Androgyne, a dancer personifies the sublime divinity—reconciliation of opposites and symbol of the original unity of life.

Three years after this initiation, while I was in the South Pacific islands of Vanuatu, photographing against the setting sun a mask used in sacred performances, my camera jammed irreparably—ending the journey with a vision as powerful as at its start.

My photographs are the closest I will ever come to conveying the immense enrichment of my meanderings through South Asia and the South Pacific. They will speak for me. In this brief introduction, I will provide only the setting and then let the "dancing spirits" begin their performances. I started my journey in 1984, following the seasons and my intuition through Bali, Java, Sumatra, Borneo, Thailand, Burma, India, and Nepal. After returning to New Zealand, my birthplace, for a brief rest, I continued on to remote regions of Australia and the Solomon and Vanuatu islands in the Pacific. I was compelled by a need to meet those people who still maintain profound spiritual bonds with the earth—the gods, goddesses, and energies of its creatures and landscapes—and affirm this connection and their own vitality through performance.

I travelled by foot, dug-out canoe, bus, and train, along razor-edged mountains, through deserts and rain forests—often feeling like a young initiate, undergoing a series of preparatory "encounters" before allowed to meet these people and see their dances. When I at last arrived, I was received with disarming intimacy. Despite the language barriers, I felt remarkable connections with the various cultures; once they heard of my interests, the villagers were usually eager to show me their performances; sensing the threat of modernity to their traditional ways, they felt that I could help assure the preservation and place of these traditions among the wisdoms of the world.

As though the journey were in progress still, I can see hundreds of children and curious onlookers streaming through fields and village streets to watch the "living spirit" dancing amidst the rice paddies or castle ruins—being photographed, at times, by the first white woman they had ever seen. These people showed and entrusted to me tremendous gifts: the dances of their creation stories, exploits of their cultural heroes, visions of their deities, rituals of the hunt, ceremonies of initiation, funerary rites—actually manifesting or becoming in the process the divine energy, sorrowful king, flying monkey hero, fearless hunter, initiated adult, ancestral voice. To these people the earth is a boundless repository of sacred power and wisdom, which may be entered into and united with through the transformative powers of dance, myth, and ritual.

The images come from various cultural and religious performance traditions, but all communicate via the language of signs—gesture, color, costume, expression—to convey a meaning that has been handed down for generations, and to lead the spectator and performer into a consciousness of life beyond the perimeters of everyday awareness. They are performances to entertain; instill moral and spiritual values in the young; preserve traditional identity; give form and expression to the subtle truths and insights of the heart; pass on local myths; establish models of perfection; commune with deities; initiate the young into knowledge of life's mysteries; maintain an equilibrium between the forces of light and shadow; assist spirits of the dead to return to their places of re-birth—and through all this to unite the performer and spectator with the divine in nature.

This book is not intended as an anthropological study. For the meaning behind the performances I consulted the works of numerous scholars; I relied primarily, however, on the people themselves to educate me. They told me the myths and fables of their clans and explained how many of the dances were "left as gifts" to them by their ancestors, or taught to them "by deities in dreams." Often these centuries-old performances have acquired varying interpretations as they passed through the generations—sometimes the dance alone is all that remains, its meaning lost entirely or carefully guarded by initiates and adepts. While it has at times been extremely difficult to attach written words to a visual and largely mute art form, I have tried to indicate

some of these many and overlapping interpretations or intentions through the captions and division of photographs into specific chapters—which move from the secular to the most sacred, or from the body of life into its soul. The image itself, however, is the preeminent messenger of the mood, symbol, and philosophy behind the performance and its culture—the words are added only as background illumination or explanation. Each photograph is clearly one moment of "stillness" within a performance, but through this single image I have hoped to relay the essential message of the performance.

Some of the performers are from the last generation to perform the ancient dances, myths, and rituals. And while certain other dances are still performed, their original spiritual function has been subsumed into spectacle as the performers have moved from temple to stage. In some instances I sought to recapture the power of the intended environmental settings and asked the performers to leave their elevated platforms and return to the earth to dance; this was only achieved with their approval. But modernization, which has discouraged indigenous traditions as "backward" and allowed highways to cut through sacred mountains; democracy, which has put an end to royal patronage of dancers; and the advent of missionaries, who tried, often successfully, to outlaw tribal "heathenisms" have all weakened traditional bonds. Despite this relentless chiselling away, much of the dance, myth, and ritual of these people has survived, a testament to their astounding resilience. Some national governments have had the foresight to protect the privacy of the more fragile cultural traditions, and thus I have had to be deliberately ambiguous in identifying the locations and people of the photographs.

This is not an elegy to a dying way; as is shown through the photographs of this book, many of these cultural traditions have been kept vibrantly alive through the dance. Dance is a metaphor for life—the contemplation and sharing of its creative impulse. Its source is the dancing flame of creation and its truth, the turning circle of eternity. I hope that both the dynamism and gentleness of these people who still echo "the old ways of Earth and Spirit" through dance are mirrored, even faintly, in these pages.

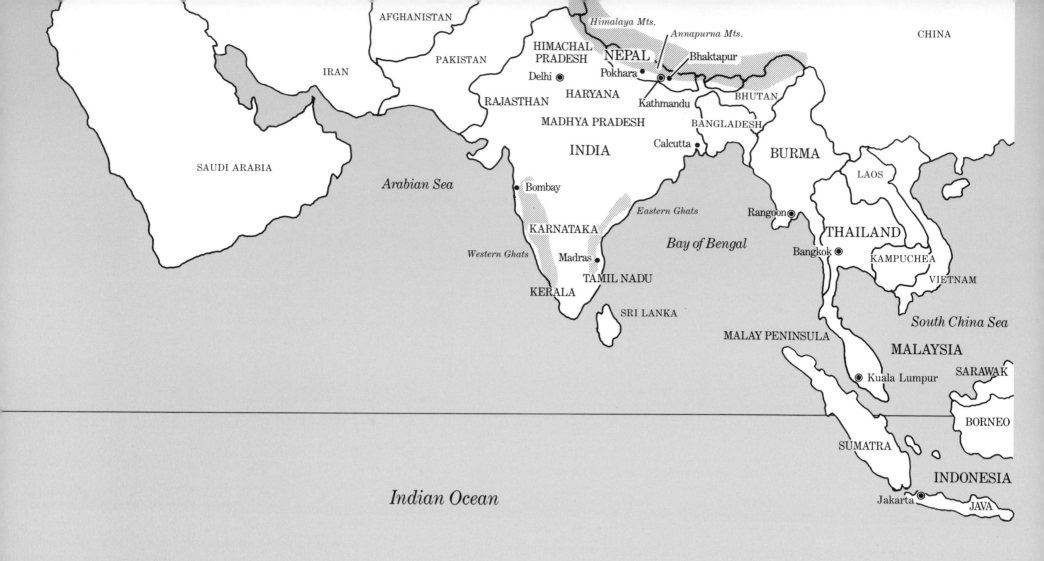

AFGHANISTAN

CHINA

IRAN

PAKISTAN

HIMACHAL
PRADESH

Himalaya Mts.

Annapurna Mts.

NEPAL

Bhaktapur

SAUDI ARABIA

Delhi ◉

Pokhara

RAJASTHAN

HARYANA

Kathmandu

BHUTAN

MADHYA PRADESH

BANGLADESH

INDIA

Calcutta

BURMA

Arabian Sea

Bombay

LAOS

Eastern Ghats

Rangoon ◉

THAILAND

KARNATAKA

Bay of Bengal

Western Ghats

Madras

Bangkok ◉

KAMPUCHEA

TAMIL NADU

VIETNAM

KERALA

SRI LANKA

South China Sea

MALAY PENINSULA

MALAYSIA

SARAWAK

Kuala Lumpur ◉

BORNEO

SUMATRA

INDONESIA

Indian Ocean

Jakarta ◉

JAVA

THE STORYTELLERS

Perhaps the most accessible and universal medium of communication, dance is used by traditional cultures as a visual form of storytelling. Meaning is conveyed through movement of the body, facial expression, gestures of the hands, often accompanied by music and song—rather than via the elaborate costumes or masks seen in more sacred performances. The images of this chapter dwell in the secular realm, illustrating the spontaneous and playful spirit of the dance, and its place within the heart and hearth of a community.

The performances here range from pure dance images, abstractions of emotions, to lessons in local mores, narratives of tribal folklore, and village celebrations. A Polynesian woman expresses with quiet dignity the pride she feels for her deceased husband; a *bhawai* dancer travels through the villages of Rajasthan with a stack of pots several feet high on his head, relaying by his act of perfect balance the message that all goals may be achieved through dedication. More literal performances tell of historic events or tribal legends, bringing to life ancient figures and thus preserving local history and wisdoms of the past. Such narratives often carry moral lessons, which are impressed upon the viewer through the subtlety of the art form.

Some performances are simply scenes from traditional life—a celebration of freedom from daily chores, a gentle mockery through caricature of an eccentric local figure or familiar animal. In the dance of the Indian milkmaid a young performer enacts the part of an imaginary woman who plans to secretly meet her lover, while on her way to milk the cows. Although performed as pure entertainment, dance of this kind also exposes the desire for forbidden, romantic love in a society of arranged marriages, and thus makes light of social tensions existing between private desires and traditional customs, rather than leaving them to fester beneath the surface of a community. The performers, delighting in the spirit of the dance, bring to life the stories and traditions of a people, preserving them and their teachings for the next generation.

Opposite and following: The tribal Aborigines of Australia trace their spiritual and cultural origins back to the exploits of creator heroes, who travelled the land during a mythical Dreamtime, or pre-time. As they journeyed across the featureless land, the heroes gave it form, embellishing the horizon with mountains, valleys, rivers, rocks. They sang and danced about the phenomena they encountered, transforming them, in the process, into the life forms of historical time. These creation sites, or "places of the Dreamings," subsequently became the totemic centers or sacred story places of particular Aboriginal clans. The journeys—Dreamings—of the creator heroes are ritualistically re-lived in song and dance. As a preparation for their eventual initiation into the sacred knowledge and power of the Dreamings, children learn of the "secular spirit" of their environment and the inter-dependence of all life forms through non-sacred story dance. Wearing the totemic insignia of their clan—the spots, "seafoam" and the lines, "rainbow"— uninitiated boys dance the stories of the creatures with whom they live: the mud-shell sisters (a shellfish found in nearby lagoons) and flat-faced crow (a local bird). They perform in the place where "stingray" and "turtle" were transformed during the Dreamtime into two rocks—one directly behind the children, the other in the ocean beyond.
North Queensland, Australia

Above and opposite: Unlike sacred performance, Yoi or "play dance" is not restricted to a particular time or event and thus allows for spontaneity and general conviviality. The animals with whom these people share their environment often become figures of fun: here, Tiwi women mimic the characteristics of (above) "buffalo sitting down," (opposite, clockwise) "lady wallabies going to the water hole," "airplane bird buzzing in the sky," "dog," and "crocodile creeping along the mud bank."
Bathurst Island, Australia

26

Opposite: A Polynesian woman performs Hai Tangi, a song of lament, admiration, and pride for her deceased husband. She is the last of her race to wear the Tu'u, a mark of maturation, tattooed on her arms and chest. The central line of the tattoo is said to derive from a dark line along the spine of a shark and to have been worn by the sky god Tehainga'atua. On the woman's breasts are the marks of a sacred fish—the bonito; the tattoos on her legs indicate that she is of a high social rank.

While centuries ago Bellonese women played central roles in *sacred rituals and dances, they were gradually excluded and have turned instead to the quiet, dignified expression of more personal emotions through song and dance.*
Bellona, Solomon Islands

Above: Giroha, a women's play dance, draws its musical accompaniment from the synchronized thwacking of halved coconut shells on the surface of the water. The dance is an occasion for women from this district of Makira to be together and enjoy respite from their work.
Makira, Solomon Islands

Above and opposite: Women of Santa Ana re-enact the celebration of Mwaque—or the payment of red-shell money which they have been given in return for providing young men with entertainment. The occasion for this festivity arises when a local "big man" requires work or building to be done around his village compound. To encourage volunteers among the young men of the village, an invitation is sent out to women of a nearby compound, asking them to assist with the work by entertaining the laborers. When the work is completed the "big man"

pays the women for their services and they return home to celebrate their gains.
Natagera, Santa Ana, Solomon Islands

Opposite and above: Villagers of Malaita re-enact a tribal story of the dreaded one-legged, one-eyed giant—or dodore. *Warned by a messenger bird of the arrival of this fearful entity, the townspeople gathered together into a circle so as to appear larger than life and scare the giant away. This tactic backfired, however, as it simply provided the* dodore *with a larger selection of food from which to choose.*
Malaita, Solomon Islands

Left and opposite: The dances of the Adivasi, or "first people," of Madhya Pradesh were originally linked to the planting and hunting of food, but are today primarily an expression of togetherness and high spirits, enhanced by the consumption of palm wine, the native liquor of this region. Although traditionally a jungle-dwelling people, these particular Adivasi are settled near a government outpost and survive by hunting and the cultivation of crops.
Madhya Pradesh, India

Following: A Jogi woman dances in front of her beautifully painted adobe home. These desert nomads possess neither property nor social position, but live as outcasts on barren land that provides no more than subsistence. Despite their bleak environment, the indomitable artistic spirit of the Jogi finds expression in dance and the decoration of their temporary homes. Among the traditional motifs painted on the adobe walls is the swastika, an ancient Sanskrit emblem.
Rajasthan, India

Opposite: Beseeching her chaperone not to tell on her, a milkmaid prepares to secretly meet her lover; and above, a young wife warns her domineering mother-in-law to keep her distance. While performed as pure entertainment, story dances of this kind help to diffuse tensions in a society that does not recognize personal choice or romantic love as determining factors in marriage. Haryana, India

Following: The pot dancer, or bhawai, earns a living by performing his dance in village streets or at country fairs. He balances on his head a stack of pots several feet high in a display of perfect balance. His skill conveys the message that all goals can be reached through dedication. Rajasthan, India

Opposite and above: The puppet dance is a popular tradition in southern Asia; shadow puppets and marionettes, or rod puppets, mimic with eerie accuracy the human characters they portray, while the human "puppet" dancers are judged by their ability to convincingly recreate the movements of puppets. The dancers, whether human or brought to life by a puppeteer's skill, often re-enact popular tales from the Ramayana *und* Mahabharata *epics, or, as in this case, the* Jatakas, *which recount the stories of Buddha's previous incarnations. Such dances are generally concerned with the virtuous life and carry with them moral lessons.*
Rangoon, Burma

*Opposite: The classical legong dance was an art form developed by the Hindu-Balinese royalty as an accoutrement to their entourage. Young girls were selected from local villages and taken into royal courts to be trained in this highly demanding, abstract dance form. With the disintegration of the court system early in this century, the legong dancers were re-absorbed into the villages where they continue to perform today, transforming themselves into the characters of court dramas—gods, goddesses, demons, sorrowful queens, romantic kings—perpetuating both the stories of the past and the moral lessons inherent in them.
Bali, Indonesia*

*Right and following: During the hot, back-breaking hours in the rice paddies, frogs help alleviate the monotony of the day by providing entertainment with their boisterous lovemaking. The village people repeat the antics of these paddy-dwelling creatures through theatrical mimicry, going so far as to create elaborate love dramas around frog life.
Bali, Indonesia*

Opposite: *Two Nepalese dancers, playing husband and wife, perform a Tibetan folk dance in Chinese traditional costume. A cultural hybrid, this dance reflects the intermingling of various eastern Asian traditions. The dance is intended to show the intimacy of the married state—although here, it is ironically performed by two men.*
Pokhara, Nepal

Above: *At harvest time, young Akha girls from Northern Thailand don new clothes and perform their courtship dance. The performance—a vigorous, circular hopping dance—is designed to provoke shy girls into laughter and thus reveal their inherent beauty to potential suitors.*
North Thailand

Above: Children born in lands
where dance is recognized as the
expression of the soul as
well as the embodiment of life
learn to dance when they learn to
walk.
Pokhara, Nepal

Opposite and following: These two
dances are performed by Tibetan
refugees living in Nepal. The
actions of the performer at the
right are a spontaneous reaction to
the presence of a bull nearby. On
the following pages, a Tibetan
gypsy performs a good luck dance;
the unifying symbols of the sun
and moon—light and dark—are
incorporated into his mask and
costume.
Pokhara, Nepal

Opposite and above: In a traditional Maori custom, the afterbirth, or whenua, of a new-born is buried between the earth and roots of a tree to ensure that the child is connected to the life force, or mauri, of the Earth Mother, and to affirm the relationship existing between the Earth Mother and humanity. Through this act, the tree becomes the child's life symbol and here, in the shadows of such a tree, a mother expresses through song and gesture a message to her son, "Oh my child, my love for you will never die..."
North Island, New Zealand

ARCHETYPES OF CULTURE

The heroic monkey general Hanuman opens the chapter soaring through the air, displaying the legendary powers of this revered mythical creature. He is a hero by virtue of his consummate loyalty, honesty, and courage—and is graced with gravity-defying powers and the ability to heal, among his many attributes. He joins the other heroes, healers, warriors, hunters, kings, queens, chiefs, and priests of this chapter in the splendid pantheon of divinely-inspired ideal models. Drawn from myth, history, religion, the inner sanctums of the spirit, contemporary figures and events, these characters are both dancers personifying, and in some instances actually embodying, aspects of perfection—spiritual and physical beauty, grace, strength, truth—and serve as vivid representations of the human aspiration to the divine.

The exalted status of the performer or character portrayed may have been inherited (such as the position of tribal chief and king) or achieved through meditation, undivided allegiance to a divine energy, excellence in combat or the arts, display of an extraordinary ability, initiation, possession of a sacred object, or imitation of the dress and manner of local deities. Costumes and their accoutrements play a more important role here than in the previous chapter as they assist in expressing the divine aesthetic.

Among these models of integrity and leadership are their opposites, the fallen leaders—spiritual and emotional inverts. These negative figures, such as the power-hungry prime minister or witch widow, displayed here through theatrical caricature, visual abstraction, and pantomimic re-enactment, represent contrasting elements of the personality, and serve as striking examples of the perversions of power and the corruption, through ignorance or avarice, of beauty, strength, and grace. The conflict between these opposing forces is made manifest at the close of the chapter, where the light, gentle powers of the personality are challenged by shadowy, violent, powers in a dramatic Solomon Island performance.

While the characters seen in this chapter are often partnered with, or act as vessels for, gods and spirits, they are not themselves considered divine (such divinities appear in the final chapter of the book). Models of perfection—whose physical qualities reflect their spiritual state—these archetypes protect and perpetuate a people's identity with all that is best in their culture.

Opposite and following: One of the oldest of the Indian epics, the Ramayana *tells of the adventures of Rama, "the gentle one" and incarnation of the Hindu god Vishnu. When Rama's noble wife Sita was abducted by the demon Ravana, Rama called on the monkey general Hanuman (opposite and following), the monkey king Sugriva (page 64), and Jambava the bear king (page 65) for help. With the assistance of the natural energies of life, symbolized by these animal heroes, Rama conquered the demon king, rescued his wife, and saw that order was returned to the universe. Characters from the centuries-old* Ramayana *are still revered today in India and other Hindu countries. The three heroes—Hanuman, Sugriva, and Jambava—belong to the Golden Age, when, according to Hindu mythology, the deities walked upon the earth and all creatures—human and animal—shared the same speech.*
Bali, Indonesia

Above, opposite, and preceding:
Child of the monkey queen and
Vayu the wind god, the Hindu
monkey hero Hanuman possesses
the power of flight, the ability to
change size at will, to disappear, to
uplift mountains, and to heal.
Also a servant, Hanuman
symbolizes the qualities of loyalty
and selflessness.
Here, and on the previous page, a
Balinese dancer embodying the
monkey hero exhibits some of his
attributes.
Bali, Indonesia

*Two characters from the Hindu
Ramayana: Sugriva, king of the
monkeys (above), is a protector of
animals and the terrestrial realm;
through the power of his pure
animal energy, the bear king
Jambava (opposite) can single-
handedly vanquish marauding
demons.
Both characters have been
immortalized in the stories of the
Ramayana as symbols of the
beneficent powers within nature.
Here, dancers in southern India
keep alive the ancient poetry of the
epic—its lessons and wisdoms.
This performance, in the*

*Yaksagana style or "music of the
heavenly beings," differs from
other Indian traditions as it relies
on speech rather than elaborate
gesture.
Karnataka, India*

*Opposite and above: At the
entrance to a Hindu temple—or
threshold to the eternal—a Baris
dancer manifests himself as the
invincible animal power, "king of
the tigers." The Baris, a
militaristic style of dance,
exemplifies strong, masculine
elegance and is the source material
for all Balinese male dances.
Bali, Indonesia*

Left: Classical Javanese dance-drama was cultivated in royal courts as an expression of control and refinement in accordance with aristocratic ideals. Until recently, the highly stylized dances were performed by royalty or members of the aristocracy. The dancers personify archetypes of mortal perfection—beauty, grace, dignity—and form role models of Javanese culture. These physical ideals are in essence qualities of the spirit, made manifest through the aesthetics of Javanese classical dance.
Here, a princess in the posture of adornment, checks herself in an imaginary mirror. The dancer performs in the topeng tradition—or dance-drama with masks; the whiteness of her mask symbolizes spiritual purity.
Java, Indonesia

Opposite: Endowed with invincible power from the magical kris—a serpentine dagger—two young Baris dancers stand ready to fight. The kris, which brings death to those it strikes, is a representational embodiment of the great naga, or snake—symbol of the life-sustaining waters.
Bali, Indonesia

Kirana insisted that she was truly herself, clearly the soul of Angreni had entered the princess so as to be forever close to Panji.

In these tales Panji (right) is identified with the ideal male. His spiritual and physical grace, control, and dignity are reflected in his excellence both in battle and the arts. As the archetype of mortal perfection, his character is said to "shine like the sun." His counterpart, the princess (left), in turn, represents the feminine ideal. Chandra Kirana, or "the radiant ray of the moon" is also compared to light, but hers is a softer light that gives peace, as does the moon. It is said that the story surrounding the love affair of this couple is in fact the age-old myth of the sun and moon in eternal pursuit of each other. The gesture of the female dancer signifies an act of beautification—both inward and outward.
Java, Indonesia

Above and opposite: Many of the Javanese models for behavior are drawn from local mythology. The Panji cycle—a series of stories revolving around the exploits of the semi-mythical culture-hero Panji—has been a particularly fertile source. Here, and in the following pages, dancers re-enact the stories from this series and in so doing reinforce and perpetuate the ideals of Javanese culture.
The stories comprising the Panji cycle came into existence in East Java during the 12th and 13th centuries, in the time of the two kingdoms of Jenggala and Katiri.

As a child, the young prince Panji of the Jenggala kingdom was engaged to his cousin, Chandra Kirana of Katiri. The two cousins, however, never met, and the young Panji fell in love with another woman, Angreni. Their affair endangered the long-standing peace between the two kingdoms, so Panji's father had the beautiful Angreni killed. Panji was crazed with grief but eventually realized he had to honor the family pledge. Upon meeting his betrothed, at long last, he immediately recognized in her his first love, Angreni. Although Chandra

Flicking her scarf to echo her feminine qualities of weightlessness and flight, Princess Ragil Kuning (left),awaits her lover, the prince Gunung Sari (opposite). In anticipation of meeting the princess, Gunung studies his male grace reflected in the royal pool. Unlike the love affair of their brother and sister, Panji and Chandra Kirana, the love of these two is considered unrefined as the lovers are too talkative.
Java, Indonesia

Following: Dance of the Garudas, the giant eagles who symbolize the sun. This heroic, mythic bird was adopted by the Thai royal family as their insignia.
North Thailand

Opposite: In the stories of the Javanese prince Panji, Klono "the wanderer" was a foreign king who entered Java in order to win the hand of Princess Chandra Kirana, having fallen in love with her image in his dreams. He came to Java, besotted, to pursue the princess, but his passion for her was so obsessive that he eventually lost all sense of himself.
A king, whose regal office granted him the position of semi-divinity, Klono lost his dignity and eventually his life to the devouring force of lust. The dancer portraying King Klono wears a red mask—color of raw emotions; his gestures indicate that he is in search of his love.
Java, Indonesia

Above: A dancer assumes the countenance and stance of a king in a courtly Javanese tradition called wayang-wong, *or dance-drama without masks.*
Java, Indonesia

handsome that he risks being seduced by the Inelwa, a group of female deities. To prevent mortals and immortals from mixing in this way, men must be seen in pairs during the ceremony.

The men performing wear ornaments of shell and croton leaves, a highly fragrant plant. The cloth on the lower body is woven from banana fibers by the men on back-strap looms. The knee/calf rattles make percussive noises as the men stamp out the rhythms of their songs. Parts of the Nala dress, particularly the shell and coral ornaments, are passed down through the generations, maintaining bonds with the deities and the traditional culture learned from them.

Santa Cruz, Solomon Islands

Opposite: The fish living in the salt waters of the old man are his property. No one is allowed to hunt for them without his permission, a law that is obeyed by all except the spirit world. Hungry and homeless, ghosts are constant thieves; to prevent these intruders from robbing him, the old man prepares to confront them. Dressed in the colors of his spirit self, the man guards his fish (represented by the two children), and waits for the ghosts to appear.

Vao, Vanuatu

Above and following: A long time ago, during the days when human beings were ignorant of culture, deities living in chambers beneath the ocean surfaced and came to land to perform their rituals. At the sound of their strange singing, the human inhabitants crept forward, and by spying on the deities, learned how to dress and dance.

Now, whenever misfortune strikes a village of Santa Cruz, men summon deities to their aid by imitating them in the "Nala" costume and dance. However, this imitation makes a man so

Pages 84–85: The image on the left is a representation of a Maori chief as he would have appeared early in the last century, during the first days of the British influence in New Zealand. His costume combines European and traditional dress. The full-face tattoo reflects the position and mana *(power) of his standing. Maori leadership is based on primogeniture, whereby the eldest—male or female—in a ruling family is regarded as the primary person of the tribe. By nature of this exalted birth, a chief is referred to as* taumata, *or "resting place of the gods," and his or her* mana *is considered to be the greatest in society.*

The feather cloak was originally made to suit the mana *of its owner. Women fashioned these cloaks, chanting prayers as they did so. The prayers, called* karakia, *were implanted in the cloak, imbuing it with their powers. The* karakia *are still used today in many tribal activities and create a continuum between the secular and sacred aspects of life.*

The moko, *or facial tattoo, was prevalent among Maori men and women until British colonization of New Zealand and the arrival of Christian missionaries in the 19th century. An essential part of traditional culture, the* moko *served as a personal signature, indicating the social and spiritual status of the wearer. The image on the right depicts a modern, engraved* moko *combining graffiti with traditional design. Among the motifs are the forehead lines—three sets denoting experience in warfare (top), skill in oration (center), and knowledge of genealogy (bottom). The spiral motif, displayed in part, is taken from the frond of a native fern as a regenerative symbol.*

North Island, New Zealand

Above and opposite: As paramount chief and high priest of this mountainous region, Inarobo ("holder of shell money") Aumanu ("dancing birds") is semi-divine. Endowed with the powers of his office, he watches over the transition of the mortal into the immortal, that is, from death into ancestral spirit. This act is considered the spiritual counterpart to the birth-giving power of women—albeit a superior power, according to the men of the region.

Malaita, Solomon Islands

Buddhist drama is unusual; only a person capable of elevating the consciousness of another to a higher state would be forgiven for the murder. Here, in killing the king the monk liberated him from his evil, a truth echoed by the repentant dying words of the king: "Oh, why was I not killed three years ago to save me from committing so much sin?"
Himachal Pradesh, India

Following: To the desert dacoits, or mischief makers, who wander about the land causing trouble, male prowess is synonymous with the sword. Here, a dacoit performing a sword dance asserts his masculinity.
The man shown here was later killed; having beheaded a number of his enemies, he eventually lost his own head to another's blade.
Rajasthan, India

Opposite: Ekalavya is the invincible king of the hunters, the great archer whom only the gods can kill. He appears in the Mahabharata, *the great epic containing many of the religious teachings and archetypes of the Indian spiritual foundation.*
Karnataka, India

Above: After arranging the murder of his older brother, the evil king Lang Darma ascended the throne of Tibet (c. A.D. 896). He persecuted the monastic order of lamas, desecrating their temples and burning their sacred texts in an attempt to uproot the Buddhist religion. For three years terror reigned until a monk named Palgyi Dorje obeyed a vision. He appeared at a public event, wearing the loose-fitting black robe and hat characteristic of the pre-Buddhist Bon "devil dancers" of Tibet. The king, watching from a balcony high above the crowds, became interested in the dancing figure below and motioned to him to approach; the monk obeyed, drawing a bow and arrow from the ample sleeves of his robe, and with one shot killed the malevolent king. The taking of a life in a

Above and opposite: The leyaks, or psychic vampires, are the most fearsome of Balinese beings. Diseased in spirit, they are living people who have allied themselves to the forces of evil by deliberately reversing the positive energies of the psyche. They are known to meet at crossroads and in cemeteries, where they perform rituals enabling them to become changelings, such as animals or ghouls. Their identity hidden, they seek out those fatigued by emotional strain—as from bereavement—and attack these people, draining them of their remaining life force.

This stage performance, which gives theatrical form to the creatures, is based on the 16th-century legend of Rangda the witch widow and devotee of the dark goddess, Durga. The character portrayed here is Creluluk, the "prime minister" of Rangda's legion of leyaks.

Bali, Indonesia

90

Left: Clowns often appear in Balinese dance-dramas amid serious battles between good and evil. Here, frustrated by the inconclusiveness of the battle, two clowns draw their swords to determine the victor themselves. The half-masks used by the clowns indicate their limbo position—part-human, part-divine. The light-hearted touch they bring to social life transforms the serious into entertainment. They also feature in religious activities where the laughter they induce gives joy to the deities.
Bali, Indonesia

Opposite: With the license to ridicule and caricature, clowns in Balinese theatre keep social values in balance. Here, one depicts the bulging eyes and wide grin of a prime minister as he greedily surveys his dominions. Entering into what should be the heroic realm of high political office, the clown shows the archetype corrupted by lust for power.
Bali, Indonesia

Above: A stylized form of self defense, pencak-silat *derives its combative stances from the gestures of animals: enraged monkeys, flying storks, tigers, snakes, swallows, as well as the more unlikely movements of weaving drunkards and newborn babies. In mastering this art, the performer obtains the powers of mental telepathy and mystic healing through touch.*
Sumatra, Indonesia

Opposite and following: Mako-mako Ai-matauwa (to cover one's self with mud) Ai-fono-fono (the

coming of a people from afar) is an ancient drama involving a gentle, light-skinned, tree-dwelling and tree-worshipping people who came to a violent end when they were invaded and massacred by a dark-skinned, sea-faring people. On one level this performance re-enacts their story; on another it contrasts the light and gentle with the dark and destructive aspects of the personality—or the difference between the ideal and the despised. Still another interpretation follows on the next page.
Natagera, Santa Ana, Solomon Islands

Preceding, opposite, and above: In cultures with no written traditions, generations-old performances often acquire several different stories or interpretations—each of them true, in its way, to the spirit of the original performance. Another story behind this re-enactment tells of a warrior party of cannibals who came to hunt human flesh. Aware of their danger, the hunted people covered themselves in mud to appear as if spirits. Upon seeing this transformation, the killers were stopped in their tracks, until one of the the younger "spirits" tripped while disappearing into the jungle, giving away the disguise. Natagera, Santa Ana, Solomon Islands

COMMUNION AND TRANSFORMATION

High in the Annapurna mountains of Nepal, a woman performs a dance-ritual to the creative and nurturing powers of the mountain goddess Parvati. This goddess is perceived to be present in all women and thus the performer obliquely acknowledges her own powers of creation—the divinity in herself. During this consuming worship, as in all such rituals, the distinction between the goddess and the woman blurs; the creatrix and created merge.

Through the transformative capacities of ritual—worship, trance, purification, initiation—the performers of this chapter seek to commune with the energies and spirits of the land and soul, invoking and often absorbing their magnificence. Instruction in the performance of traditional ritual usually begins at puberty with the first initiation ceremonies. These spiritual rites of passage then continue on throughout a lifetime, often as a series of complex ritual cycles designed to introduce the initiates into a knowledge of the mysteries and wisdoms of their inheritance.

Although Aborigine children are taught early on about ancestry and their place within the scheme of life, they are not granted entry into the spiritual powers of the Dreamings—the sacred beliefs and stories of their clans—until a ritual initiation into the "ecstatic" state. Fishermen of Santa Ana in the Solomon Islands must undergo a "baptismal" initiation involving immersion in the blood of the bonito fish, before acquiring the power to capture the fish. Such ritual performances mark transition points in a person's life—or the life of a community, as for example, a dance performed to rid a village of sickness or exorcise malevolent energies. But rituals are also an integral part of everyday activities in traditional cultures. To those who live off the land, food often possesses sacred qualities because of its life-giving powers. Ritual-dances are performed to encourage fertility in the land, arouse the spirit of the coconut, merge with the essence of the bonito fish.

These rituals continue on to death and beyond, helping spirits of the deceased return to their totemic centers and the life-cycle to continue, as in the closing image of the chapter.

With the first light of day, as the dawn mists rise to hide the Annapurna mountains, a celebrant of the Hindu women's festival Tij Barata performs her puja, or worship. Beginning on the 5th day of the brightening moon, Tij is celebrated by women in honor of the goddess Parvati, "the mountaineer" who mobilized the creative energies of the cosmos with her seduction of the reclusive, ascetic male principle, the god Shiva.
Present in all women, Parvati is one of the approachable forms of Devi, the female force of Creation. She is embodied in the earth as mistress of The Himalaya, where she has her throne, and the goddess Annapurna—or "she who is full of nourishment"—after whom the Annapurna mountains are named. The Himalaya, Nepal

Following: As spring arrives, Bheel Gameti women are granted social dominance for a few days and emerge in vibrant color to acknowledge and celebrate life's potency in the Ghoomra, a ritualistic "dance of renewal."
Rajasthan, India

Opposite: Dressed as a woman, a man imitates the dance of the spheres in the Thali, or dish dance. The circular dish is a symbol of unity and when two dishes are placed together in this ritualistic dance, they signify the union of the sexes and the knowledge of infinity that comes from this intimacy.
Rajasthan, India

Above: Amidst the ruins of Jaisalmer Castle, wandering bards, or Pabuji bhopas *("voices of the deities"), relive in song and dance the exploits and life of the founder of their religious and* social culture, the deified folk hero, Pabu. This bhopa *performs in front of a large painted scroll which depicts the 15th-century hero and his deeds.*
A ritualistic performance unaltered for centuries, the art of this desert people displays not only the spiritual bonds they maintain with the founder of their religion but the way in which traditional dance serves as a living history of a culture.
Rajasthan, India

Following: In Vedic Hindu mythology, the horse was one of the ten precious things to be born from the transformation of the milk ocean into the salt water ocean at the time of creation. At the end of this present Hindu age of Kali Yuga, Kalki the white horse—a term descriptive of the ocean's waves—will appear as the tenth incarnation of Vishnu, preserver of life.
Invoking the powers of the horse through identification with this ancient symbol, trance dancers are able to perform rituals of divination and exorcism. While still a feature of temple activities in many areas, the dummy horse dance has become largely a secular one.
Tamil Nadu, India

Opposite and above: An expression of the union of the individual soul with the universal soul, dance is also the revelation of the divine essence dwelling within a person. In South India, the dance considered to be the ultimate manifestation of these truths is the Bharata Natyam.
Requiring years of devotion and training, the Bharata Natyam is based on an ancient devotional dance once performed in temples by women called devadasis, or "dancers of the deities." As religious dancers, the devadasis were considered to hold the key to *the experience of religious ecstasy. Today, the Bharata Natyam continues to communicate via the symbolic language of movement once used by the devadasi to reveal wisdoms of the soul.*
Tamil Nadu, India

Opposite and above: Sitting cross-legged in a circle the ketjak, *or monkey chorus dancers, wove their bodies back and forth in increasingly trance-like rhythms until they metamorphosed into monkeys. The dance was performed at the convergence of two rivers, an area recognized by Balinese to be full of power as it is here that supernatural energies carried by the waters tumbling from the sacred mountains are known to congregate.*
The "monkey dance" performed today is part-theatrical representation, part-ritual in *which the "white monkey god" collects the mystic energies— symbolized by fire—into the vortex of the* ketjaks' *circle. Traditionally this would have accompanied a ritualistic trance dance used to exorcise malevolent energies from the land.*
Bali, India

Above: Encircled by dancing bodies, conch blowers signal the arrival of Ataro si Fenua—"spirits of the land"—in whose honor the Wagosia ritual is performed. These spirits pass through the village with the conch choir and cleanse it of its ills. At the end of the ceremony, women carry the conches out to sea and, shouting to the spirits, instruct them to remove all sickness and filth from their community and unload it elsewhere.
Santa Ana, Solomon Islands

Opposite and following: Among the last of the Santa Ana fishermen to have been initiatied into the sacred hunt, men throw out metaphorical nets in a performance involving the capture of the bonito fish.
Santa Ana, Solomon Islands

Opposite, above, and preceding:
The bonito, or albacore tuna, is the
traditional and once sacred food
source of the people of this island.
Sacred for its blood and
association with the supernatural,
the bonito was a cornerstone of
local religion and male initiation
rites until these traditions were
supplanted by Christianity.
The perilous fishing of the deep-sea
bonito far off the shores of Santa
Ana was considered the domain of
men. Before allowed into the trade,
fishermen had to be ritually united
with the spirit of the fish through
initiation at puberty involving

immersion in and drinking of the
sacred bonito blood. While these
initiation rituals, as well as
traditional methods of fishing, are
no longer practised today, the
performance here is a remnant of
this former way of life and still
contains a degree of its sacred
element.
Santa Ana, Solomon Islands

Page 120: Objects such as the one held by the man at the left reflect the spiritual and social status of a person, achieved by progressing through various stages of rituals. Performed throughout a man's lifetime and swathed in secrecy, the rituals include the absorption of the soul of a sacrificial animal and symbolic rebirth; via these steps, a man gradually attains sanctification and immortality.
Malekula, Vanuatu

Page 121: The color red is associated among many Aboriginal Australians with the hues of sunset—and blood, symbolizing both death and rebirth. The Tiwi people of northern Australia attribute transformative powers to this color found in the earth and stones. Ochre is used here as body paint during the Kolema ceremony—an initiation ritual linked to the harvesting of yams, an island staple.
Bathurst Island, Australia

Above: In traditional cultures, food often possesses sacred qualities because of its life-giving properties. The coconut, one of the staples of many traditional South Pacific people, holds a dominant place in local religions. Here, the Numbotanohhonewed—or "sacred custom head belonging to the coconut"—is an embodiment of the coconut spirit and used in rituals to assure the fertility of the fruit.
Malekula, Vanuatu

Opposite: Demonstrating a sacred ritual, women of Malaita prepare to eat the meat of the coconut. They carry it to a priest chief who will desacralize it, break it into pieces, and distribute it among the women for eating. A symbol of growth and nourishment among traditional cultures of the South Pacific, the coconut is considered in this region to be sacred; its mystic properties are harnessed in rites to renew the life force of ancestor spirits. During these regenerative ceremonies, the coconut is referred to as weewela, or "infant."
Malaita, Solomon Islands

Above and opposite: A man from east Arnhemland performs a private ritual song and dance in a clearing among the ghost gum trees.
Arnhemland, Australia

Opposite, right, and below: Young boys of the Daly River accompany their elders into the place of initiation. Here they will be removed from the world of childhood and ushered into the spiritual identity of their clan. With arms outstretched, mothers relinquish their bonds, while the men move in to infuse the initiates with the power of the Dreamings— the creation stories of their clan. They sing and dance these sacred stories, linking the boys now to the infiniteness of the Dreamtime cycle—the creation time of Aboriginal mythology. The ceremony, and subsequent change in spiritual and physical status, introduces a boy to adulthood and prepares him for social and marital responsibilities and the knowledge of sacred rituals. Such initiations are not as common for women, who are believed to gain power gradually through the long process of maturation, child-bearing, and daily productivity. Northern Territory, Australia

Following: Aboriginal men of the Wik society ritualistically re-enact in song and dance the exploits, or Dreamings, of their clan's creator heroes—the Pal-luuchan brothers— during the mythical Dreamtime. While travelling south across the land, the two heroes came upon "whalefish," or Aakam, who had become crippled after submerging himself in the poisonous soft mud at the edge of the ocean. The brothers sang and danced about him as he staggered around on his crutches, one brother fanning "whalefish" with his Brolga bird wing feathers to cool him down, the other acting as a bodyguard. When the brothers completed their songs and dances, "whalefish" sank down, entering the earth at Walmoerichany-nhiin, which then became the story place of the whale and a sacred site to this clan. As with all Aboriginal ritual songs and dances, the performers are not merely imitating mythical stories and characters but actually becoming the creator heroes and "whalefish," thereby incorporating the mythic past and its powers into the present. North Queensland, Australia

Opposite and above: In honor of the sky goddess Nguatupu'a and her brother Tepoutu'uinganga, men dressed in the costume of the gods perform the sacred Kapa dance. They dance on the beach where, generations ago, the deities were carried across the ocean in the form of two stones. The resting place of these sacred stones became the focal site of the local Bellonese religion until they were smashed by zealous missionaries who outlawed traditonal religious practises. Despite this, however, vestiges of the old ways can still be seen in such performances. Bellona, Solomon Islands

Next four pages: These single-, double-, and multiple-faced masks are worn during funerary rituals that involve approaching the body of the deceased. The specific meaning of the rituals are known only to the male initiates involved in the highly sacred ceremonies. However, various references to the metamorphosis of the spirit can be seen carved onto the masks: the nighthawk, or owl, a bird associated with the flight of the soul, often makes its appearance on the headdresses.
Malekula, Vanuatu

131

Opposite and above: Painted with the ochre colors of sunset and white of seafoam, old women of the Wik society perform the Wuunk Pian ritual. The ritual, performed only for deceased men, involves the return of a man's "earthly shadow" from its mortal home back to its original totemic site. The performing women, generally beyond child-bearing age, are called Ithwun-kalantan— "pregnant-belly carrying"—because they carry the man's spirit with them during the ritual. At the close of the ceremonies, the women dress in elaborate body paint (shown here) to make themselves sexually attractive, acknowledging that in death there is celebration of life, and asserting that as it is women who bring life into the world, so also is it women who dispatch the spirit back to its source.
North Queensland, Australia

THE JOURNEY

In the Hindu Golden Age or Eternal Dreamtime of Australian Aboriginal mythology, deities and spirits dwelled on and in the earth, roaming the land in the living forms of birds, fish, plants, rocks, fire, water, humans—all communicating freely with one another in a universal language. With the gradual fragmentation of this perfect unity, the deities have remained, but are no longer visible through ordinary channels of perception. Today, they are made incarnate, and their wisdoms and messages relayed, through the insights of visionaries—seers, priests, priestesses—the creative imagination, and language of the body. Here, invoked by ancient dance-rituals of humans, these ancestral spirits, energies, ghostly specters, divine or demonic powers, emerge from dwelling places in jungles, rivers, or the more interior reaches of the soul, to merge with their dancing reflections.

The spirits and deities revealed here are the culmination of ritual—images of an absolute belief. The embodiment of a devouring ghost opens the chapter in a circle of fire, guarding the entrance into an otherworldly journey. The journey is marked by wandering ghosts, supernatural entities, ambiguous deities, and abstract passions and wisdoms dwelling in the land or labyrinths of the soul. Krishna, hero of the *Mahabharata* epic, is the god embodying transcendent love; Tane, the young Maori demi-god, separated his impassioned parents, the Earth and Sky, and thus opened the way for light and life to enter the world; the two Aborigine fertility mothers, Bildjiwurajou and Murlaidj, crossed the sea and formed the first humans; Mahadevi, the Great Hindu Mother goddess possessed the key to the universe; the black-faced Lankalakshmi guarded the gates to the kingdom of demons. These beings are among the mystical forces of life, the source and meaning of culture, religion, tradition, and philosophy— creative essences of the earth-spirit.

Opposite and following pages: In areas of Vanuatu the spirit of a dead person is believed to pass through the Cave of the Dead, journeying on to join its ancestors and live in eternity with the great spirit and source of fire—the volcano Botgharambi. During the journey numerous obstacles are placed in the spirit's path, to challenge or destroy its precious essence. One of these is the guardian of the way, the devouring ghost Le-hev-hev who stands upright in a path of flames. If she does not succeed in destroying the spirit, she becomes mystically entwined with the journeying soul. This highly sacred mask symbolically resembles the devouring ghost. Although worn by a man, the gender of the mask is female and carries on it the night hawk. Nocturnal birds, particularly the owl, are regarded as "the fluttering of the spirit" as it leaves the body at sunset and begins its journey.
Malekula, Vanuatu

In Aboriginal Australia the spirit is generally thought to take three forms at death: one that returns to the person's totemic center to await re-birth; another that remains with the body and gradually fades as the body decays; and a third that travels west to the Land of the Dead.

To these Aborigines of Arnhemland, the Land of the Dead is an island across the water. Above, the raftman waits by the edge of the water to ferry over the spirit of a dead person. If the spirit is male, the raftman carries a club and beats the spirit all the way to the Land of the Dead, but if it is female, the raftman lifts her gently onto his raft and paddles slowly across the water. At the end of the journey, however, the spirit is expected to pay for the crossing with coitus. Occasionally the spirit that remains with the body does not willingly accept death but lingers about, upsetting relations between the living. Opposite, one of these resentful spirits is represented in the rain forest of Queensland.
Arnhemland and North Queensland, Australia

*Opposite: The spirits of those
who die a violent death never find
a resting place and wander as
ta-matoam—or fiery ghosts—
among the living. When walking
about at night, the living must
carry fire torches to protect
themselves from the violence of
these aggressive spirits personified
here.
Vao, Vanuatu*

Above and following: The dodores
*of North Malaita are vicious, often
one-eyed, one-legged giants,
similar to the* rhakshasa *of the
Indian* Ramayana *epic. Neither*

*human nor spirit, these giants are
particularly fierce and, although
considered today to be
semi-mythical beings, they still
have the power to evoke feelings of
dread in the villagers who
remember them from traditional
lore. The* dodore *on the following
pages is called Ahinamala—or
"leaf of a shady tree."
Local performances that portray
these beings on a pantomimic scale
instill in the young a healthy
respect for the dangers lurking in
the surrounding jungle.
Malaita, Solomon Islands*

147

Opposite and above: The kakamora
*("to go quietly") are tiny mythical
creatures who were believed to have
once existed, but now remain alive
largely in the imagination. They
lived in holes in the earth and in
trees, had long hair, and loved to
dance. Fascinated by fire, which
they did not know how to make
themselves, they stole firebrands
from humans' fires to play with. In
mythic lore they are believed to be
the progeny of the four-eyed, four-
breasted, hermaphroditic, and
winged serpent Kahausibwari.
Makira, Solomon Islands*

151

Following: During the Indra-jatra *fertility festival every spring, Indra the storm god comes down in the form of mist to penetrate the earth and fertilize the plowed fields. This is a time of great mystical potency; the regenerative energies of nature are awakened, gods and goddesses intermingle, and the spirits of the land move about, making themselves known to the community. The figures shown here are the attendants of the Mother goddess who shows herself during the festival. They are, from left to right: Bvuca the goblin, Singa the lion, Betal the spirit of chaos, Kava the skeleton. During such religious festivities, the performers act as mediums for these attendants, releasing their energies among the community. Bhaktapur, Nepal*

Opposite: Wakawakamanu or "spirit of the sea" is an ocean-dwelling creature of mysterious power. It has a dual nature, at once malevolent—shooting people with its arrows of flying fish—and kindly—as teacher of the dance. It is seen in the breaking waves and in dreams, where it appears in its kindly aspect. Wakawakamanu is represented in art as part-human, part-fish.
Makira, Solomon Islands

Above: Ancestor spirits often make their homes in hidden places on riverbanks. To retain contact with these spirits, living relations use mediums who become the "voices" of the dead ancestors through the transformative capacities of the udo, or death mask.
Sarawak, Borneo

Opposite: The Kauravas and Pandavas were two feuding families believed to live in northern India during the 1st century B.C. As told in the Mahabharata epic, the Kauravas cheated the Pandavas of their kingdom in a game of dice and inflicted further insult when Dussasana of the Kauravas (opposite), the archetypal image of vileness, assaulted a Pandava woman. The Pandavas retaliated by putting a curse of death on their enemies. The ensuing bloody battles between the two families found no relief until the god Krishna intervened, ending the conflict with his words: "All is illusion, including war and death." Many of the stories of the Mahabharata contain messages of the destructive effects of human ambition and the futility of anger and hatred.
Kerala, India

Left: Known by different names throughout Southeast Asia, Thosakan is the incarnation of demonic power. In the mythical battle in which he appears in the Ramayana epic, the hero Rama vanquishes the demon, and in so doing, recognizes Thosakan as another part of himself.
Central Thailand

*Above and opposite: The figure
with the black face is the goddess
Lankalakshmi, who lost her soul,
through a curse, to the forces of
evil and was made guardian of the
gates to the kingdom of demons.
Her salvation and the restoration
of her divinity could only be
achieved through the touch of an
animal. Hanuman, the heroic
monkey god (figure at left), on
his journey to help rescue Rama's
wife Sita from the clutches of
demons, struck Lankalakshmi,
freeing her from the curse.
Kerala, India*

Emerging from their retreat, two Tibetan Buddhist monks perform sacred dances in the courtyard of their monastery in Northern India. Opposite, Senge Dradog, the "lion-voiced guru," is the emanation of compassionate wrath. In Tibetan Tantric Buddhism, wrath is recognized as being in unity with the peaceful deities dwelling within soul. Through compassion, Tibetan Buddhists mobilize the energies of wrath against negative emotions, forcing them to turn back on themselves and dissipate. Above, a Tibetan Tantric monk dances the part of the chief deity of the mandala. The essence of this deity is empty appearance, a state of void, or the Tantric Buddhist concept of "Oneness." The masked dancer carries the eye of wisdom on his forehead; in his right hand is the bell—symbol of release and the feminine, and in his left is the vajre—symbol of the masculine principle and the immutable. These dances are manifestations of deities seen in the visions of Tantric Buddhist masters. Displaying the dances—and thus the visions—to the public is considered a great blessing. Himachal Pradesh, India

Above: A Tantric Buddhist symbol of the mind's evolution towards enlightenment, the skeletal Lord of the Cemeteries, symbol of fearlessness, appears when the blood of attachment and flesh of ignorance have fallen away, consumed by the "void"—leaving the self pure and free. The Tantric Buddhist conception of the ultimate reality is a state of being without a god, a recognition of creator and created as non-distinct—a state of void, or "Oneness." The dance is performed to evoke this level of enlightenment. Himachal Pradesh, India

Following: Garuda, king of the birds in Balinese Hindu mythology, is represented as having the head, wings, and talons of an eagle and the torso of a man. In the epic Ramayana, *Garuda roams the world fighting evil and is famous for his hatred of snakes. Although antagonists in the mythic poem, the two creatures—celestial bird, symbol of the sun and masculine principle—and terrestrial serpent, symbol of the earthly waters and female principle—together are among the fructifying elements of life. Bali, Indonesia*

Above: The forest lion or night hunter—the tiger—is the archetypal image of raw and violent power. With a fierceness that shrivels the soul, the tiger in Vedic mythology is the companion animal energy of the warrior goddess, Durga, who rides upon its back when vanquishing the destroyer of cosmic order, the demon Mahisa. Rajasthan, India

Opposite: Hanuman, monkey hero of the Ramayana *epic, here appears in his godly aspect. His acts of service to Rama, Lankalakshmi, and other characters of the epic were performed with a purity and bravery that elevated him to the realm of the divine.*
He is a symbol of primal unity and the healing powers found in nature.
Kerala, India

Above: Nandi the bull is the animal-energy and mount of Shiva, the god who "wears the moon in his hair." The moon, particularly the crescent moon, is also the symbol of Nandi (shown on the performer's forehead) and reflects the animal's original connection to the fertility Mother goddess religions of ancient India; much of the iconography of these sects has been absorbed into modern India's polytheistic Hinduism.
Karnataka, India

During the Kumari-jatra festival, Devi, the Mother goddess, appears in the body of a young virgin as the living goddess Kumari. In honor of this maternal energy, gods and their votaries present themselves to her. Included among the entourage is Krishna the entrancer, who beguiled the milkmaids with his ethereal flute playing (his blue face connotes desire) and the loyal Hanuman, identified by his red face. Kathmandu, Nepal

Opposite: *In contrast to Mahakali, the golden-skinned Lakshmi (another form of the goddess Mahadevi) is benevolent and life bestowing. Born from the Cosmic lotus, she is the goddess Earth and has as her symbol the pot—or vessel of life. Her companion, Kaumari, is also a benevolent, maternal force. Both goddesses, embodied here by religious initiates, carry the crescent moon and vegetation in their headdresses, as symbols of the feminine power of fertility. Bhaktapur, Nepal*

According to the Kena Upanishad *from the 6th century* B.C., *Mahadevi, the Great Mother goddess or woman incarnate, possessed the key to the mysteries of the universe, and it was she who initiated the male gods into the most elementary knowledge of these secrets. In her fierce aspect, Mahadevi is known as Mahakali (above), symbol of the creative violence of the Great Mother. Her blood red countenance and the sword and skull cap in her hands express the life-lust of this maternal force. In the back is a statue of the many-armed Durga*

and her companion tiger. Bhaktapur, Nepal

170

Darpanam: *"The movement of the body is the movement of the world and its speech the sum of all language. Those who are acquainted with the moods of the heart should use the hands with due care."*
Kerala, India

Following: So perpetual and deep was the passion between Rangi the Sky Father and Papa the Earth Mother that their children, lying between them, knew nothing but a never-ending darkness. One of these children, Tane-Mahuta-te-wairo, "the sunlight," grew restless with the desire for freedom, and forcing his parents apart, stepped out into the world, letting light and life enter. After creating the trees and birds, Tane ascended to the twelfth heaven to aquire two sacred stones and three baskets of knowledge containing these teachings: knowledge pertains to the head, wisdom to the heart, and illumination of the spirit comes through moho puku, or "dwelling within one's inner being."
This is a modern interpretation of the young demi-god Tane and the Maori creation myth.
Aromoana, New Zealand

Opposite and above: Both dancers perform in the Kathakali tradition, a classical story-play style of Southern India which relies on mudras, or gestures, rather than speech to relay its stories, and colors to denote its character types. The dancers' faces are painted green—color of heroic, kingly, and divine types—and they wear the sacred mark of Vishnu the Preserver on their foreheads. The figure opposite represents Krishna, the Vedic Hindu god and principle of love who came into the world to combat evil, a story that is told in the Mahabharata epic. As a young man of outstanding beauty and great musical prowess on the flute, Krishna caused all the young dairy maids to fall hopelessly in love with him. He taught that divinity could be found within the self through the gradual intensification of physical love until its eventual entry into the transcendent realm of divine love. The character personified above is Bhima, also a hero from the Mahabharata. His facial expression denotes "wonder" and the Kathakali mudra indicates this wisdom, as expressed by the Indian philosopher Abinaya

Above and opposite: According to the religious beliefs of tribal Australian Aborigines, every aspect of their lives and surroundings—animals, humans, rituals, dances, geographic sites and names, language—was formed during the mythical Dreamtime by creator heroes. These heroes, their creations, and the creation processes—the Dreamings—are inextricably linked to the constitution of an individual, forming a living part of the physical, spiritual, and social fabric of Aboriginal life. Here, an initiated Aborigine man becomes "one flesh, one spirit" with his and his clan's inherited totemic animals—"cassowary" (left) and "emu" (right) birds. Through this spiritual fusion, he enters into the knowledge of the "Eternal Dreamtime."
North Queensland, Australia

Opposite, above, and following:
Following the path of the morning
sun, the two Aboriginal fertility
mothers, Bildjiwurajou and
Muralaidj, came across the sea
with their brother Djanygawul and
his companion. Carrying sacred
dilly bags containing all the
ritualistic emblems, the two
mothers formed the first human
beings and gave life to them.
After a time their brother, his
companion, and the newly created
men grew jealous of the mothers'
sacred powers and stole the dilly
bags. Consoling one another over
their loss, the elder of the mothers

concluded: "We have really lost
nothing, because we remember it
all and we can let the men have
that small part. Aren't we still
sacred even if we have lost the
bags?" The boys, here, perform a
secular re-enactment of the myth.
Arnhemland, Australia

179

Left and opposite: This headdress contains the ancestral identities of both man (Seviehuwo) and woman (Seviemahu). It tells of the creation myth of people from this region of Vanuatu—a myth similar to one heard in parts of Australia. In the beginning, a woman owned all the sacred knowledge and culture of life, but lost it, thus losing it for all women, to a man, Seviehuwo, who bought it from her. This legend was told by the present owner of the mask.
Malekula, Vanuatu

Opposite: In parts of the Solomon Islands, women are believed to have brought both life and death into the world. A woman, here, re-enacts the story of Koevasi, a mythic female snake who gave birth to the first human—a woman. This woman, sometimes identified as the snake herself, growing old, went to the river to change her skin and regain her youth. On returning to the village, her granddaughter did not recognize her and was so afraid of the "new person" that the old woman returned to the river and, finding her old skin, put it back on—thus bringing death into the world. Figona, or snake worship, is a religious practise found in parts of the Solomon Islands, although it is now nearly extinct.
Malaita, Solomon Islands

Above: One myth of the Vanuatu Islands tells of Qat the culture hero, creator of night and sleep, who was born from the splitting of a stone. Great powers have since been attributed to stones. Thought to be the dwelling places of ancestral and guardian spirits, they are used as mediums in exorcism rituals and as sacrificial platforms and dolmens in rites of rebirth.
Vao, Vanuatu

Above and preceding: Sanghyang Tjintiya, "the divine slippery one, the one difficult to imagine or grasp hold of," preceded, in Balinese mythology, the separation of male and female—and is the divine androgyne. The oldest of the Balinese divinities, Tjintiya, represented here in meditative posture, floats over the Middle World, with fire-energy issuing from the junctions of its limbs. In Indian Hinduism Tjintiya has its equivalent in Shiva Nataraja— Lord of the Dance. The dancer personifying Tjintiya stands in the middle of a lotus pond whose flower is symbol of the Cosmic womb.
Bali, Indonesia

Bibliography

Anderson, Mary M. *The Festivals of Nepal*. London: George Allen and Unwin, 1972.

Belo, Jane. *Traditional Balinese Culture*, essays. New York: Columbia University Press, 1970.

————. Bali: *Rangda and Barong*. Seattle: University of Washington Press, 1966.

Best, Elsdon. *The Maori as He Was*. Wellington, New Zealand: Government Printer, 1952.

Berndt, Ronald Murray and Catherine H. *The World of the First Australians: Aboriginal Traditional Life*. Canberra, Australia: Aboriginal Studies Press, 1988.

Codrington, R. H. *The Melanesians: Studies in Their Anthropology and Folklore*. Oxford: Oxford University Press, 1961.

Covarrubias, Miguel. *Island of Bali*. New York: Knopf, 1937.

Devi, Ragini. *Dance Dialectics of India*. Delhi: Vikas Publications, 1972.

Eliade, Mircea. *Patterns in Comparative Religion*. New York: New American Library, 1958.

Fox, C. E. and F. H. Drew. "Beliefs and Tales of San Cristoval." *Journal of the Anthropological Institute of Great Britain and Ireland* 45 (1915): 131.

Grey, Sir George. *Polynesian Mythology*. London: Routledge, 1906.

Hooykaas, Christiaan. *Cosmogony and Creation in Balinese Tradition*. The Hague: Martinus Nijhoff, 1974.

Ivens, Walter G. *Melanesians of the South-East Solomon Islands*. London: Kegan Paul, 1927.

Keesing, Roger M. *Kwaio Religion: The Living and the Dead in a Solomon Island Society*. New York: Columbia University Press, 1982.

King, Michael. *Moko: Maori Tattooing in the 20th Century*. Wellington, New Zealand: Alister Taylor, 1972.

Kinsley, David. *Hindu Goddesses*. Berkeley, California: University of California Press, 1986.

Layard, John W. *Stone Men of Malekula*. London: Chatto and Windus, 1942.

————. "Der Mythos der Totenfahrt auf Malekula." *Eranos Jarbuch* (1937): 241.

McNeely, Jeffrey A. and Paul Spencer Wachtel. *Soul of the Tiger: Searching for Nature's Answers in Exotic Southeast Asia*. New York: Doubleday, 1988.

Mead, Sydney. *Traditional Maori Clothing*. Sydney, Australia: Reed, 1969.

Monberg, Torben. *The Religion of Bellona Island: Concepts of the Supernaturals*. Copenhagen: Nationalmuseet, 1966.

Mookerjee, Ajit. *Kali: The Feminine Force*. New York: Destiny Books, 1988.

Napier, David A. *Masks, Transformation, and Paradox*. Berkeley, California: University of California Press, 1986.

O'Flaherty, Wendy Doniger. *Women, Androgynes, and Other Mythical Beasts*. Chicago: University of Chicago Press, 1980.

Rawson, Philip. *The Art of Tantra*. Greenwich, Connecticut: New York Graphic Society, 1973.

Rossen, Jane Mink. "The Suahongi of Bellona: Polynesian Ritual Music." *Ethnomusicology* 22 (1978): 397.

Schuré, Edouard. *Krishna and Orpheus: The Great Initiates of the East and West*, translated by F. Rothwell. Chicago: Yogi Publication Society, 1908.

Slusser, Mary Shepherd. *Nepal Mandala: A Cultural Study of the Kathmandu Valley*. Princeton, New Jersey: Princeton University Press, 1982.

Tickle, L. *Taukuka: A Tattooing of the People of Bellona Island*. Honiara, Solomon Islands: Cultural Association of the Solomon Islands, 1966.

Zimmer, Heinrich. *Die Indische Weltmutter*. Frankfurt am Main: Insel, 1980.

————. *The Art of Indian Asia: Its Mythology and Transformations*, edited by Joseph Campbell. Princeton, New Jersey: Princeton University Press, 1968.

————. *Myths and Symbols in Indian Art and Civilization*, edited by Joseph Campbell. Princeton, New Jersey: Princeton University Press, 1946.

de Zoete, Beryl and Walter Spies. *Dance and Drama in Bali*. Kuala Lumpur, Malaysia: Oxford University Press, 1973.